WHEN

Does an albatross come ashore?

AF516651

Om KIDZ
An imprint of Om Books International

Contents

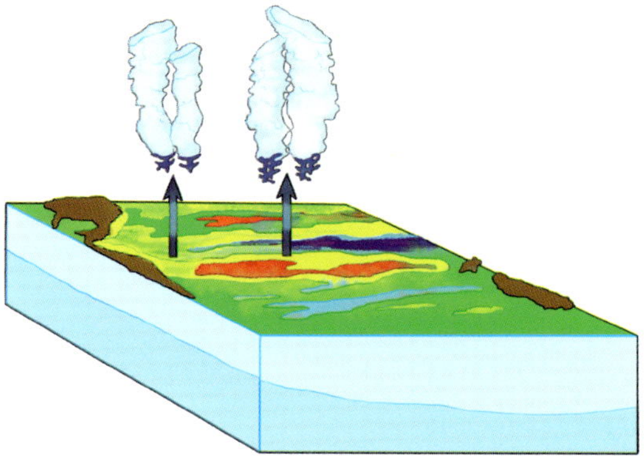

When were the oceans formed?

Billions of years ago! The oceans were formed from the escape of water vapour and other gases from the molten rocks of the Earth to the atmosphere. At that time the Earth was a hot place. Gradually, the Earth's surface had cooled to a temperature below the boiling point of water. It began to rain for a long time. As the water drained into the great hollows in the Earth's surface, the ocean came into existence!

Pocket fact

Underground ocean!
There is a huge underground ocean underneath the continent of Asia. It is of the size of the Arctic Ocean, but is all locked up inside rocks.

Try this

Which mountain range runs along the center of the ocean basins?

When was the oceanic crust formed?

Oceanic crust was formed around 200 million years ago! The oceanic crust extends 5-10 kilometres beneath the ocean floor. It is made up of different layers of rock. The rocks of the oceanic crust are often referred to as "sima." Sima stands for silicate and magnesium which are the most abundant minerals in the oceanic crust.

Rogue waves are extremely strong waves which are greater than twice the size of surrounding waves. They are often formed unexpectedly from directions other than prevailing wind and waves. Rogue waves usually occur when waves formed by a storm develop in a water current against the normal wave direction. This results in a shortening of the wave frequency and cause the waves to dynamically join together, forming very big 'rogue' waves.

Pocket fact

Digitally recorded!

A 26-metre wave struck the Draupner oil rig in the North Sea off Norway on 1 January 1995. This was one of the first observations of a Rogue wave with a digital instrument.

Find out

Who named Rossby waves?

When do Rossby Waves occur?

Rossby waves are waves that occur largely due to the Earth's rotation. These waves are formed when polar air moves towards the Equator while tropical air is moving towards the poles. The temperature at the Equator is higher than that at the poles due to differences in the amounts of solar radiation received. Thus, heat flows from low to high latitudes causing Rossby waves by these air movements.

When do tides occur?

Every day! Tides are the rise and fall of the levels of the ocean. They are caused by the gravitational pull of the Moon and Sun as well as the rotation of the Earth. The cycle of tides occurs in five steps- the rising of sea level, the occurrence of high tide, the fall in sea level, occurrence of low tide and rising of sea level again. This cycle can happen once or twice a day depending on the location of the area to the Moon.

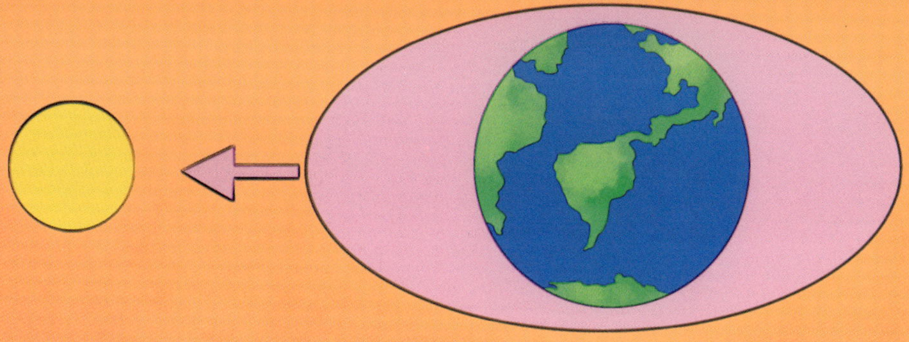

Pocket fact

Tractive Force!
During the 1100s when Latin translation interpreted their findings, Muslim astronomers formed the basis of the understanding of tides in Medieval times.

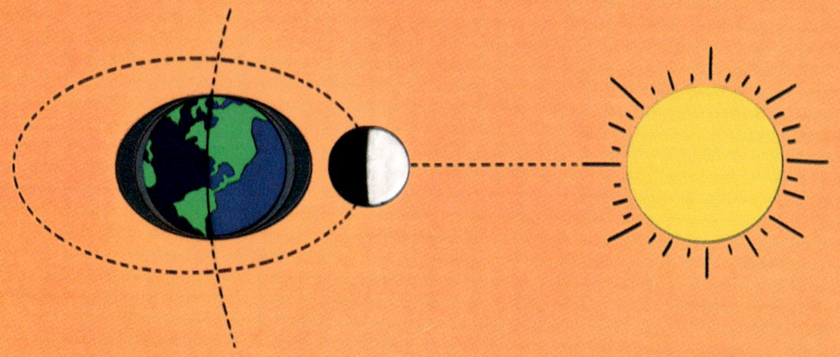

Find out

What is Spring Tide?

When do King Tides occur?

King Tide is a popular term often used to describe exceptionally high tides. These are caused when the Sun and the Moon are the closest to the Earth. When the Moon is closest to the Earth (called perigee) it has greater influence on tides. When the Sun is closest to the Earth (called perihelion) it also exerts high gravitational pull on the Earth. So when the Sun, Moon and Earth line up at perigee and perihelion, which happens twice each year, the gravitational force on the Earth is strongest, creating the King Tides.

When are currents in the ocean formed?

Ocean currents can be caused by wind, density differences in water bodies, gravity, and events such as earthquakes. When wind blows continually in a particular direction, the wind stress on the sea surface causes the water in the upper layer to move and thus, a current is formed. These wind-induced currents may be permanent in regions of strong prevailing winds.

Pocket fact

Eddy Franklin

Eddy, that formed in the Gulf of Mexico in June 2010, is named Eddy Franklin after Ben Franklin. He is known to have done research on the Gulf Stream.

Find out

Do ocean currents influence the climate? How?

When is an eddy formed?

An eddy is a circular current of water. The ocean is a huge water body that is constantly in motion. General patterns of ocean flow are called currents. Eddies are formed when small parts of these currents break off from the main body and travel independently. They can form in almost any part of a current, but are prominent in western boundary currents.

When is a storm called a hurricane?

A hurricane is a type of storm which forms over tropical or subtropical waters. When storms produce winds of 119 kilometers per hour or higher, they are called hurricanes. A hurricane has 3 parts—eye, eye wall and rain band. The eye is the hole at the centre, the eye wall is a ring of thunderstorms that swirl around the eye and the band of clouds and rain stretch for hundreds of miles.

Find out

When did hurricane Katrina occur?

Pocket fact

Let's name it!

Cyclones are named by a six-year rotating list of names. This list is updated and maintained by the World Meteorological Organization and is used to identify these storms.

When do tropical cyclones occur?

They occur at different times in different places. Tropical cyclones occur in the western North Pacific region from May to November. The Caribbean cyclone season runs from June 1 to November 30, peaking in August and September. The cyclones in South Pacific and Australia normally occur from November to April. In the Bay of Bengal and Arabian Sea, cyclone season runs from April to June, and September to November. The East Coast of Africa normally experiences tropical cyclones from November to April.

When does it snow in the ocean?

It occurs when shower of organic material falls from upper waters to the deep ocean! When plants and animals near the surface of the ocean die and decay, they fall towards the seafloor. It is just like leaves and decaying material falling from trees. This decaying material is known as "marine snow" because it looks a little bit like white fluffy bits. In addition to dead animals and plants, marine snow also includes sand, soot and other inorganic dust!

Find out

What measures can be taken to control ghost fishing?

Pocket fact

I named it!

The term 'marine snow' was first coined by the explorer William Beebe as he observed it from his bathysphere.

When does ghost fishing occur?

Ghost fishing occurs when fish and other marine animals are caught in abandoned nets. Sometimes fishing nets are discarded, lost or abandoned in the seas and oceans. When these nets get entangled on fragile coral reefs, they strangulate them. The nets can also drift in the ocean, trapping marine animals and killing them. They also act as an obstacle to navigation.

When does algal bloom occur?

Algae are photosynthetic microorganisms that are found in most aquatic habitats. An algal bloom occurs when nutrient pollution and lots of sunlight create a rapid increase in the density of the algae. When there's an algal bloom, the stream, river, lake, or ocean becomes covered with algae, creating a thick mat of surface scum. This thick layer of algae blocks sunlight from reaching the water underneath the surface, which affects the organisms living there.

Find out

When was Red Tide first recorded officially?

Pocket fact

An important role!
Algae play a significant role in the aquatic ecosystems. They serve as food for many fish and provide shelter for various animals.

When does a red tide occur?

A red tide is a common term used for a harmful algal bloom. It occurs when algae known as dinoflagellates grow in very large number, creating an algal bloom. When millions of these microscopic algae reproduce and cluster in one area of the ocean, they can change the colour of the water to a rusty shade of red. The colour may also range from pink or orange to brown or yellow.

When does coral bleaching occur?

Corals are invertebrate marine animals belonging to a large group of colourful animals called Cnidaria. Corals get their colour from tiny algae that live in their tissues. But when corals are stressed by changes in conditions such as temperature, light, or nutrients, they expel the algae living in their tissues. This causes them to turn completely white. This is called coral bleaching.

Find out

How many kinds of coral reefs are there? Name them.

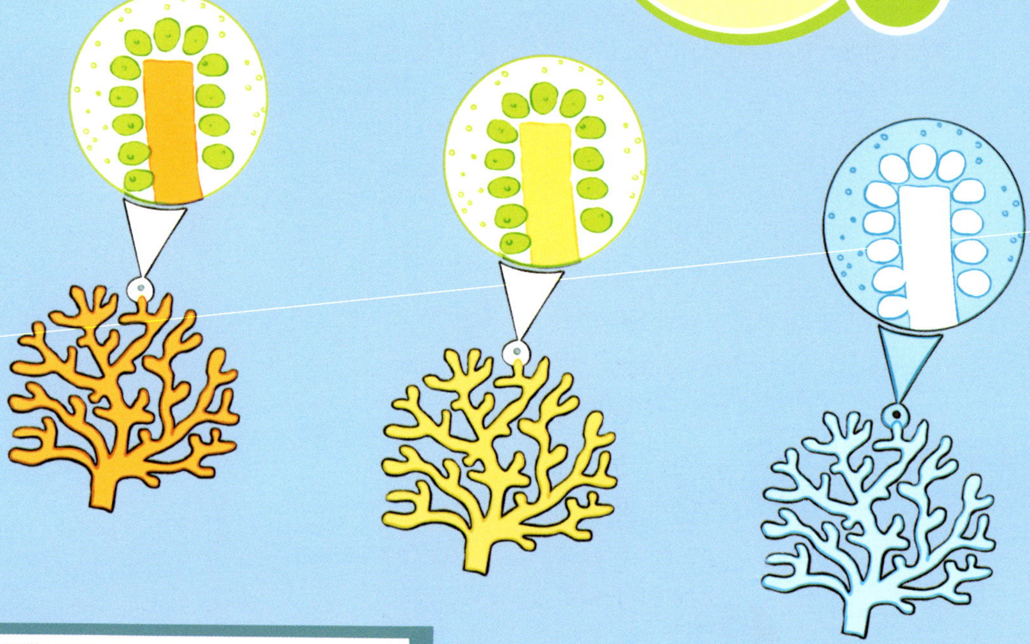

Pocket fact

The biggest wingspan!
The Wandering albatross has the biggest wingspan in the world of birds. It has a wingspan of 11 feet.

When does an albatross come ashore?

Albatrosses are among the world's largest seabirds. They are most frequently seen in the oceans of the Southern Hemisphere and in the North Pacific Ocean. They can stay aloft in windy weather for hours without ever flapping their extremely long, narrow wings. Albatrosses come ashore only to breed. This activity occurs in colonies that are usually located on remote oceanic islands.

When do fish climb ladders?

When they migrate! Many fish species migrate up and down rivers to adapt to the changing habitat. But dams, culverts, and waterfalls slow or stop fish migration. A fish ladder is a structure that allows migrating fish passage over or around such obstacles. The ladder has a series of rising pools which fish reach by swimming against a stream of water. Fish leap through the flow of rushing water, rest in a pool and then repeat the process until they are out of the ladder!

Pocket fact

My sleeping bag!
The parrot fish is known for secreting a "sleeping bag" made of jelly-like mucus. When it's time to rest, parrot fish surround themselves with this jelly to protect from predators.

Find out

Are saltwater fish different from freshwater fish?

When do fish sleep?

Fish can sleep at any time during the day or night. Their sleep is not exactly like human sleep, though. It is more like a resting period in which fish reduce their activity and metabolism while remaining alert to danger. Some fish float, some hold themselves into a secure spot in the mud or coral, and some even locate a suitable nest!

When does El Niño occur?

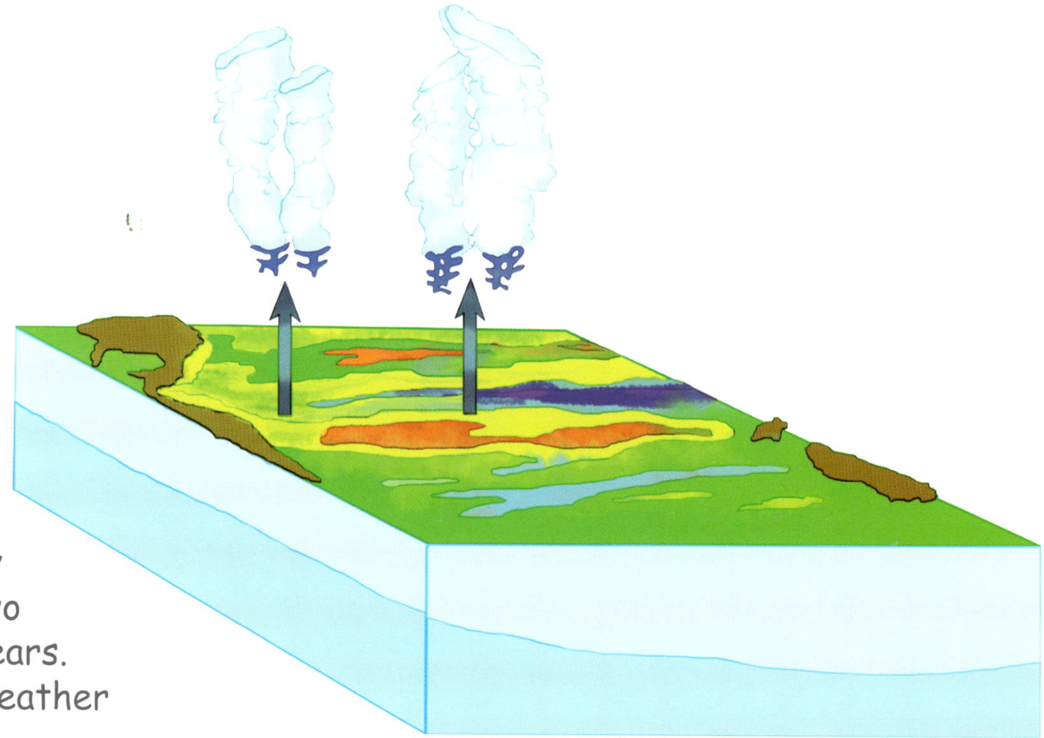

El Niño is a climate cycle in the Pacific Ocean. The cycle begins when warm water in the western tropical Pacific Ocean shifts eastward along the equator towards the coast of South America. El Niños usually occur every three to five years. They may also come as frequently as every two years or as rarely as every seven years. The El Niño also has an impact on weather patterns globally.

Pocket fact

How was it named?
The name 'Nemo' comes from Captain Nemo, a character in Jules Verne's Twenty Thousand Leagues under the Sea.

Find out

What is the Spanish name for El Niño?

When was Point Nemo first discovered?

In 1992! Point Nemo is the most remote point in the ocean. It lies in the South Pacific Ocean. Point Nemo isn't an actual 'point' as there's no land. It is simply a spot in the ocean that is around 2,688 kilometers from the nearest land. It was discovered in 1992 by a Croatian-Canadian survey engineer called Hrvoje Lukatela who used a geospatial computer program to find Point Nemo.

When were knots used to measure the speed of ships?

In the 17th century, sailors measured the speed of their ship by using a device called a "common log." It was a coil of rope with knots at equal distances, attached to a wooden panel. Sailors would throw the panel into the sea, behind the ship, and the rope would start unwinding from the reel. The faster the ship moved forward, the faster the rope would unwind. By counting the number of knots that went overboard in a given time interval, sailors could tell the speed of ships.

Pocket fact

Underwater robots!
A fleet of underwater robots was descended into Atlantic coastal waters from Nova Scotia to Georgia to collect data. It was believed that this data may help improve storm intensity forecasts for future hurricane seasons.

Find out

How is the speed of ship measured in modern times?

When was the ocean glider invented?

An ocean glider is an autonomous underwater vehicle used to collect ocean data. The concept of underwater gliders was first explored in the early 1960s. It was only by 2003 that a working thermal-powered glider, Slocum Thermal was invented. Ocean gliders require little or no human assistance while travelling. These are uniquely suited for collecting data in remote locations, safely and at relatively low cost.

When do storm surges occur?

A storm surge is the abnormal rise in seawater level during a storm. It usually occurs when a storm's winds push water onshore. A storm surge consists of very high waves and high water levels. Storm surges can occur at any time of the year and can be quite damaging in icy waters of winter.

> **Pocket fact**
>
> **The most destructive!**
> Katrina was one of the most destructive hurricanes in the history of the United States.

When do turbidity currents occur?

A turbidity current is a fast, downhill flow of water. It is caused by increased density due to high amounts of sediment. Turbidity currents can occur when there are earthquakes, collapsing slopes, and other geological disturbances. When turbid currents rush downward, they can change the physical shape of the seafloor.

> **Find out**
>
> How are turbidity currents measured?

When was the first scientific map of ocean floor created?

In the late 1970s! In olden days, sailors made maps of sea routes. These helped them define, explain, and navigate their way through the world. The first scientific map of the entire ocean floor was created by an American geologist and oceanographic cartographer Marie Tharp and her colleague Bruce Heezen. Tharp's map showed the presence of the Mid-Atlantic Ridge. This led to acceptance of the theories of plate tectonics and continental drift.

Try this!

How do sea maps help oceanographers?

Pocket fact

A large volume!

The Gulf Stream transports nearly four billion cubic feet of water per second. This is greater than the water carried by all of the world's rivers combined.

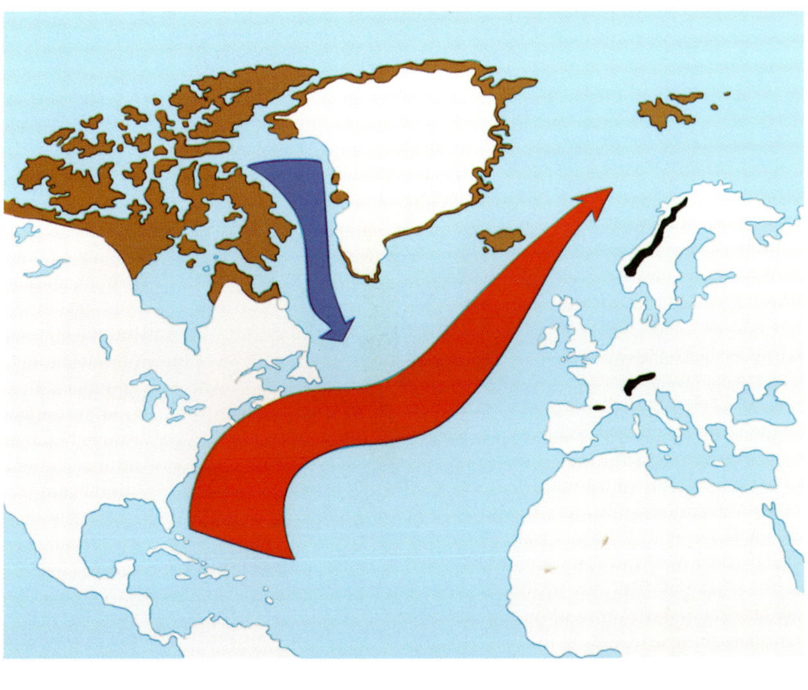

When was the Gulf Stream charted?

The Gulf Stream is a powerful current in the Atlantic Ocean. It starts in the Gulf of Mexico and flows into the Atlantic at the tip of Florida. The Gulf Stream was first mentioned by Juan Ponce de León on an expedition in 1513. It was Benjamin Franklin who first charted the Gulf Stream and published its map in 1769.

Index